WHAT IS MY

BACKYARD

MADE OF?

Written by
ALEX HALL

MATERIALS AT HOME

Library of Congress Control Number:
The Library of Congress Control Number is available on the Library of Congress website.

ISBN
979-8-89359-427-0 (library bound)
979-8-89359-447-8 (paperback)
979-8-89359-485-0 (epub)
979-8-89359-467-6 (hosted ebook)

Printed in the United States of America
Mankato, MN
012026

sales@northstareditions.com
888-417-0195

Written by:
Alex Hall

Edited by:
Noah Leatherland

Designed by:
Amy Li

PHOTO CREDITS

ALL IMAGES ARE COURTESY OF SHUTTERSTOCK.COM, UNLESS OTHERWISE STATED.
Recurring – fire_fly, xnova. Cover – domnitsky, Waridsar, Paul Maguire, photka. 4–5 – FamVeld, OlegRi. 6–7 – Kitreel, photka, SatawatK. 8–9 – bogubogu, domnitsky, Smile Studio AP. 10–11 – MagicMore, Nadezhda Zaitceva, RHJPhtotos. 12–13 – Ammak, Cmspic, katarinag. 14–15 – Gorodenkoff, Maminami, Taigi. 16–17 – Evelyn Joubert, Steve Cymro, Yes058 Montree Nanta. 18–19 – Diana Taliun, Fabrizio Guarisco, myboys.me. 20–21 – Hellotica, Richard Peterson, Sever180, Tompet, Ton Photographer, wk1003mike. 22–23 – Geber86, Jihan Nafiaa Zahri.

CONTENTS

Words that look like **this** can be found in the glossary on page 24.

WHAT ARE MATERIALS?

There are many things that you can see and touch in your backyard. These things are known as objects. Objects are made of materials. Materials can be natural or made by humans.

Wood is a natural material that comes from trees.

All materials have properties. Properties are ways of describing what something is like. Materials can be soft or hard. Some materials can be tough or weak. Materials can have many different properties.

Let's see what my backyard is made of!

MY TABLE

WOOD

My table in my backyard is made of wood. Wood is a natural material. It is strong and durable. It can last a long time if it is cared for well.

Wood can be weather resistant. If wood is stained, sealed, or painted, it can be better protected against direct sunshine and pouring rain.

MY WALL

The wall in my backyard made of bricks. Bricks are made from natural materials. They are very strong and hard. Bricks are a good building material because of their strength.

FACT: Many houses are built using bricks.

BRICK

Bricks are joined together with mortar. Mortar is a thick paste that is spread on bricks to stick them together. The mortar dries and adds to the strength of the bricks around it.

MY WIND CHIMES

My wind chimes are made of a metal called aluminum. Aluminum is a natural material. It is lightweight. This helps the wind chimes easily blow in the wind.

ALUMINUM

Aluminum resonates when struck, which means it makes a long sound when it's hit. When the wind blows the chimes, the metal tubes hit each other. They create sounds.

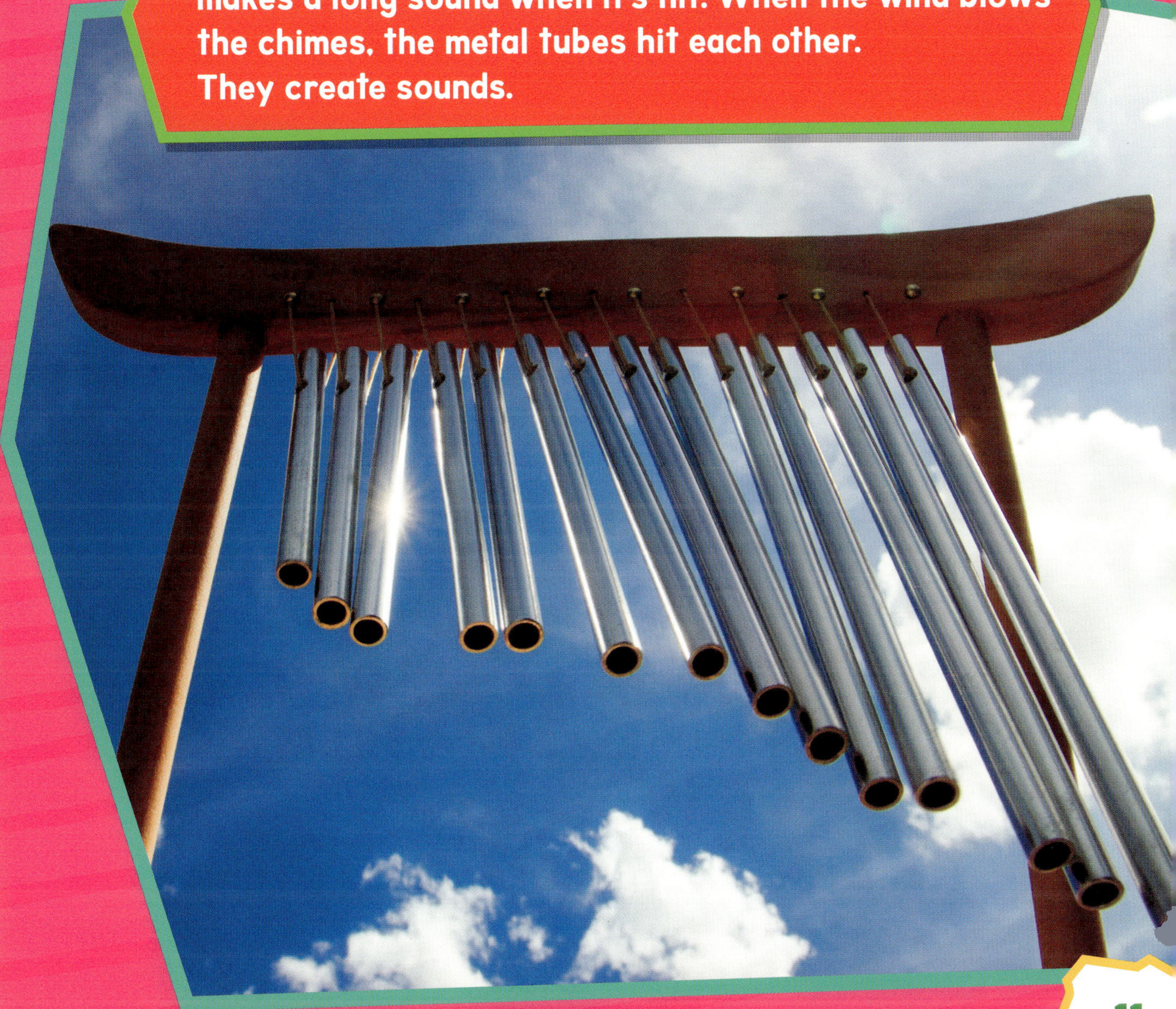

MY PATIO

CONCRETE

My patio is made of concrete slabs. Concrete is a mixture of natural materials, including gravel and sand. It is mixed with water to create a smooth paste. Concrete becomes very hard when it dries.

Concrete is strong enough to have a lot of weight on it without it cracking. This is why patio furniture can sit on concrete without damaging it. Concrete is also resistant to most weather.

MY

SWING

POLYESTER FIBERS

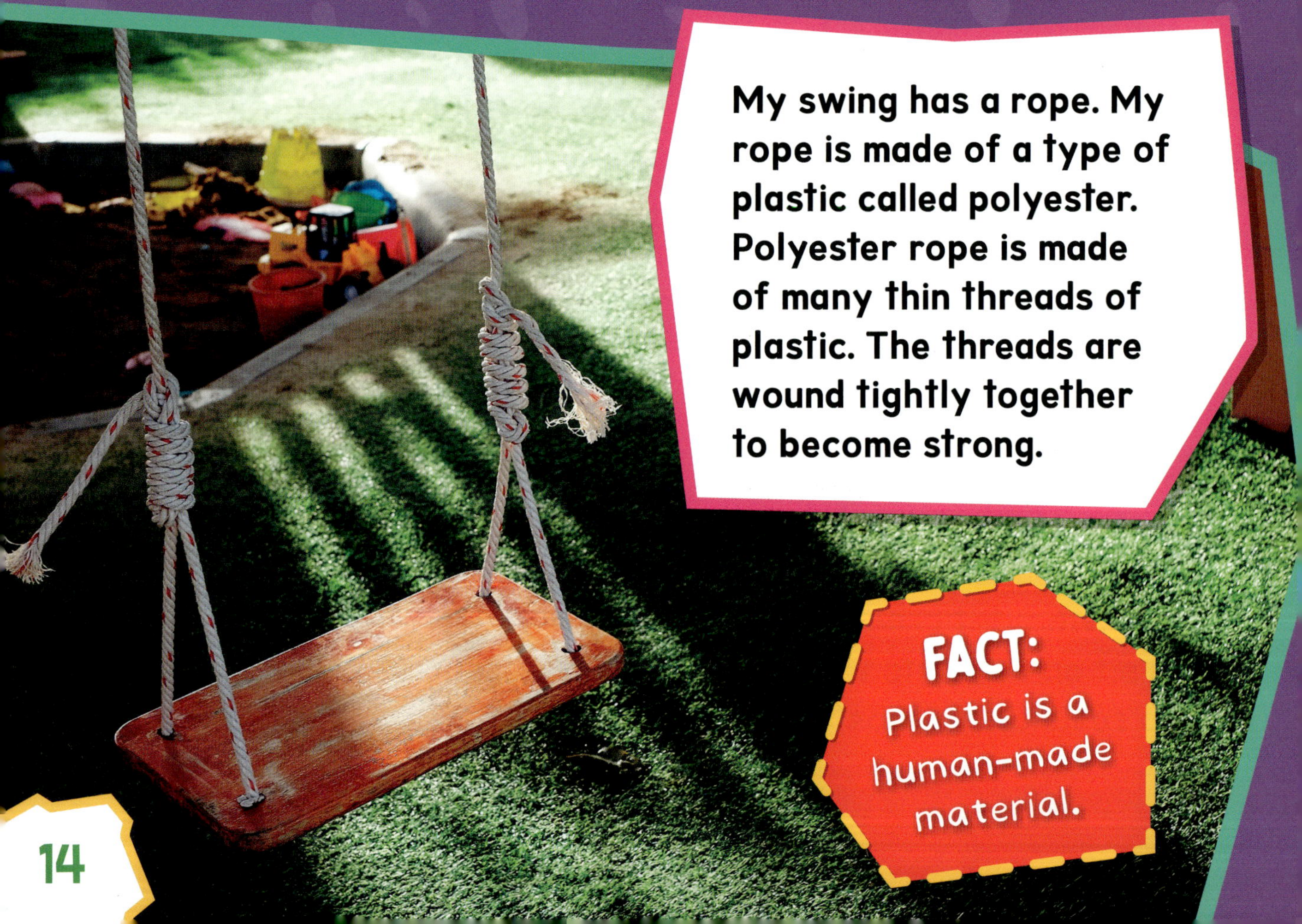

My swing has a rope. My rope is made of a type of plastic called polyester. Polyester rope is made of many thin threads of plastic. The threads are wound tightly together to become strong.

FACT:
Plastic is a human-made material.

Polyester can be flexible. A polyester rope can be pulled and bent without snapping. Its **surface** is easy to grip. Kids can hold on to the rope to stay on the swing.

MY BIRDBATH

My birdbath is made of stone. Stone is a natural material. It's hard and durable. Certain types of stone can withstand many types of weather in the garden.

STONE

Stone is very heavy. The weight of it helps keep the birdbath stable. Birds can land on it safely. Strong winds can't easily knock it over.

MY PLANT POT

My plant pot is made of clay. Clay is a natural material. The clay is made into the shape of the pot, then cooked to become hard. Clay is fragile. It can easily break.

CLAY

The surface of clay is porous. It's covered with very small gaps that we can't see. These gaps let air and **moisture** reach the soil inside, which helps plants grow.

SPOT THE MATERIALS

Which of these objects is made of plastic?

SHOVEL

GRILL

HOSE

Only the hose is made of plastic. The grill and the shovel are made of metal.

Which of these objects is made of wood?

WHEELBARROW

WATERING CAN

FENCE

Only the fence is made of wood. The watering can is made of plastic, and the wheelbarrow is made of metal.

WHAT IS IN YOUR BACKYARD?

The different materials in my backyard were chosen because of their useful properties. The materials' properties help the objects do their jobs in the backyard.

Your backyard might have similar objects to mine. They might be made of many different materials. Look at something in your backyard. What is it made of? Why was that material chosen?

GLOSSARY

DESCRIBING saying what something is like

DURABLE not easily broken or worn out

MOISTURE a small amount of liquid, such as water, that makes something wet or moist

NATURAL found in nature and not made by people

PASTE a soft, thick substance made by mixing things with a liquid such as water

SURFACE the outside or top layer of something

INDEX